$\mathcal{N}$arek-

A Path Of Perfection

The Teaching of The Armenian Church

Analysis

By Anna Anahit Paitian

Saint Gregor Narekatsi was a bishop and monk, born in Vaspuracan, ancient Armenia[1], X A.D[2].

He is a doctor of the Armenian Church, persecuted and exiled, living hidden in the mountains for his entire life, for presenting the teaching of the Chalcedon Council, 451 A.D, which was rejected by the political extraneous sacerdotal authority.

One time a hostile band of priests came to visit St Gregory to his cave during the Lent, and seeing the fried pigeons on the saint's table, they said.

- Don't you fast, Holy Father? We see meat on your table. The saint, who had provoked them intentionally, exclaimed.

- O yes, indeed, I forgot it is a fast season! - and then turning to the cooked pigeons, he said, "Now you may fly away!"

Instantly the cooked pigeons were animated and flew away alive, leaving the spectators in a great awe.

Saint Gregory Narekatsi had left his theological Catholic Orthodox inheritance; many canticles, hymns, analysis of the Holy Scripture, "The Manuscriptus of Tragedy," or "The Lamentaion Book," or, in short, as the Armenian nation calls it – "Narek" - a work, which is a greatest penitential textbook honored for centuries , in which the evil tree (universal sin) is depicted as it is in every human; the author is adopting the sins of mankind as his own, presenting them in penitential tragedy as an account to God, asking for Christ's redemptive grace for himself and all mankind.

The anatomy of the human soul and the path of perfection- all is in Narek with mathematical exactness.

A greatest book ever written by man!

---

[1] Currently- modern Turkey.
[2] 951 – 1003

The Teaching of The Armenian Church

From the Scholastic Works of
Anna Anahit Paitian

Theological analysis of

The Spirit of Narek

"The Book of Lamentation,"
St. Gregory Narekatsi,
X AD

Table Of Contents;

Preamble

It is not easy to analyze the spirit of Narek, a prayer book of St. Gregory Narekatsi, "The Book of Lamentation" (X A.D).

Many see it as a rich reservoir of vocabulary, brilliant poetic verses, exclusive style of most sublime feelings. And many even have no clue what is really Narek about, not only- they present it as inane repetitive monologues.

Only those who are capable of sincere prayers, who have cleaned own heart and make a honest effort to follow the holy monk's penitential path, only those can penetrate the mystery of Narek, a Prayer Book of a great value, for all time.

It is a time when we all should construct our own version of truths on the *absolute truth* in honesty and fervor.

It is such a joy, that Anna Anahit Paitian could discern this great literary ecclesiastical medieval jewel, presenting its clear-sighted iconic image to us, which can lead us to perfection.

This analysis is a hard scholastic research, which can direct our vision and steps toward the true objectives.

St. Gregory Narekatsi had written his manuscript as a prayer book, and it belongs to the mankind, to all nationalities; it is a book which can direct anyone to God, people from any class, everywhere, anytime.

From the Depths Of The Heart A Word to God—this is how St. Gregory starts every prayer segment.

Anna Anahit Paitian brings up the essence of this salutary book, which accomplishes our salvation by integrating our inner emotional world with doctrinal infallible formulas.

My only wish is that this exceptional work of Narek analysis could reach all, appropriated by all, for it contains the theology of created soul taught be the Creator Himself.

Father Saac Keshishian,
Monastic priest, Theologian, Translator of Narek from
the original to French,
1991, Yerevan.

I was converted to the holy faith from the atheistic destructive lies after I read Narek, witnessing great miracles.

And the greatest miracle of all is to recognize sin and to hate it.

Narek is a textbook teaching a perfection, taking me to it step by step,

it is a staircase, which takes my spirit up with every prayer clause,

it is a clean mirror reflecting myself and God,

it is a perfect image of myself in God.

From the Author

"I am a poor man with no defense, with broken heart, with troubled soul, always errant, always fallen-gambling with my heart " (Narek, Word 26:2).

In Simple Faith, In Pure Heart, In Sincere Joy

Introduction

The "Book of Lamentation", or Narek, written by St. Gregory Narekatsi, is a compass of the theological teaching of the Armenian Church, presenting the doctrinal alpha and omega of founding apostolic fathers, and it is a living baptismal pool, where we can renew ourselves in rebirth, being closer to the image of Christ, having a touchtone of the spiritual perfection. That perfection consists in one thing only; the cognition of our nature versus the nature of God, and through it the process of adoption as a new being in Christ.

Narek is possible to understand only by living it, as the saintly author says about this book being *his living body and soul.*

The whole book is about the interval enclosed between our first cry and the last gasp. That interval is presented as a *tragedy*. The tragedy of being born and alive, because the life is a drama of ongoing trials, which no one is exempt of, and which no one can pass with justification .

Our conscience is due – and it is an inherited faculty .

Our conscience can be dead, and it is an acquired faculty.

Jesus Christ is our conscience, who keeps us alive, and our regeneration as a perfect human is possible only through Him.

St. Gregory is not only a penitent individual. He presents the entire mankind in the last judgment started right now- untimely, taking from God all blessings through his humble appeal, through proclamation of his liabilities, asking to be released from.

Narek is a Purgatory and Hell, and Narek has a miraculous power to neutralize both.

Narek,Through the Baptism and Confirmation

What is a sin?

It is our weaknesses, when we give ourselves up to them.

What is weakness?

It is the absence of will to inure the nature, which is a fallen nature, the absence of the will and consciousness to sublimate our human nature according to our calling – defined by our Creator.

Narek is a furnace, where our supernatural bread is being baked against our daily bread, when we make this happen , "'Man shall not live on bread alone, but on every word that comes from the mouth of God." [3]

From the depths of the heart a word to God -this St Gregory's presentment is a word coming from the heart of men, which has one intention only; to confirm the Word of God and to live It as a Way, Truth, and Life[4].

These last three divine entities are the components of the human genius architectural complex, presented as worship- a Church. It has the basement, the pillars, and the dome with a crucifix.

St. Gregory constructs this temple inside himself, inside us. And unless we are united to this architecture – we can not keep our baptismal grace alive.

Our ways to be established in truth to be alive in Christ.

Our steps to be directed to righteousness to attain Christ.

The basement of our inner temple is our will, its pillars are apostles, its dome is Christ with His Crucifix. And this consists the essence of the baptism and confirmation, as the inner mystery connected to outer sacramental forms. This prayer book can not profit anybody, if it is not read in the humble spirit, for the entire worship of God can be only accomplished by the spirit of humility, i.e. our capacity to approach

---

[3]Matthew 4:4

[4] John 14:6

ourselves under the spiritual light of God, dissecting our souls and examining them with divine properties.

Word 88, 2[5]

"Accept the contexture of my wretched heart disrobed and exposed-
Accept this intellectual offering as a sacrifice drained of blood,
Bless and purify every word of this manuscript of laments,
Verify and confirm it as an eternal monument pleasing You.
Let my words be uttered in front of Your Throne by the class of angels,
Incensed and anointed, as a treasure for Your Treasury,
Let it be announced to all nations, to all people-
Let it be a seal of sanctity to preserve the human nature from decay –
And even though I, as a mortal, one day will not be around – I will be immortal through this Manuscript of Men with a signature of human race –
May Your will be to keep it immaculate – as it is; a condemnatory, a purgatory-
Which truly brings up all my vices without bias,

---

[5] Translations of Narek are from original Armenian and through the contemporary Armenian by Vazgen Gevorkyan, to English by the author. Presented the abbreviated versions.

Ruthlessly exposing my true self, who I am truly,
All my deeds and thoughts imperfect and erratic,
which are wrangling my heart and mind with incisive remorse,
My conscience ever- in its heartbreaking ordeal,
Let this condemnatory be as an atrocious publisher of my all human deeds working against You and my own self-
And let the whole world to know about them
As a trumpeted evil-
which I am.

I leave behind this Book of Tragedy,
I leave behind no secrets,
I leave behind no disused thoughts-
I exposed even my swaddling cloths –
Only through this scrupulous assay
Snares and ambushes of the evil will be identified and destroyed –
Leaving behind but the pile of my dried bones-
Which I trust in You, o my Lord Christ-
May Your procreating breath revives them again –
And let them to sprout and thrive in Your perennial grace!
To You, o Savior , with Your Spirit and Your Father-
United One Kingdom- absolute and inexplicable;
Holy Trinity, glory to You,
And all my adorations to You-
Forever and ever! Amen. "

Tabernacle ; Litanea

In the ecclesiastical universal ethics *litanea* is a prayer style consisting in repetitive "mea culpa, mea culpa, mea culpa[6]" – as it is in Eastern Orthodox Church, which is called "Jesus' Prayer" – a repetitive plea to be forgiven, and as it is the Rosary of the Western Church, which is a repetitive plea for the Virgin Mary's intersession.

The same way, Narek is composed of repetitive prayer sections, which present the inner system of human capability – all of it, with vices and virtues, weaknesses and strengths.

Human life is not self-standing. It is connected with spiritual powers, and we are given a freedom to make a choice. These powers are two in natures; good (absolute), and bad (absolute), both developing on their own paths to be *absolute*; a *way-truth –life*, or a *way-deception-death.*

The spiritual religious life of the individual is about invoking these spirits.

In vocabulary terms, the Armenian classic language uses special words to define these spirits, reserving *Spirit- hnqh-* for the Holy Spirit , and *sprite (spright)* – *nqh* for fallen souls, be it men's or demons.

From here *spiritual* means the worship of a true God, which can be only *through humility and penance.*

---

[6] "I have sinned" in Latin.

And *sprigtal* means a worship of low cosmic energies (powers) in gayety, in earthly joy, which are turned into fetishes. And we see now this kind of worship in Protestant and Vatican II faux Catholic churches.

The same way in Islam, or Oriental pagan religions they use *mantras* *to* invoke these spirit-s*pights*, which are being present upon the invocation, and which have a commission to serve the worshiper, elevating him to the deceptive *Trans*, to be transformed as *a fetish* himself.

The opposite process is the orthodox worship, during which the Holy Spirit is being invoked by; a) humility and self-analysis discovering the net of sins, forming **the consciousness,** awareness of sin (weaknesses),

b)humility and self-analysis, forming the consciousness of God's holiness.

Each prayer- chapter of Narek does enclose these two; self-analysis and glorification of God, which generates a perfection in human, and it is *the **recognition** of the Trinitarian true and only God-* the dogmatic (divine-infallible) formula of the Father-Son-Holy Spirit.

Narek is presenting a *Woe* and *Glory*, the first one is reserved to men, the second one – to God, and every chapter is a stair of a ladder taking up to the éclat of the redeemed man, led by these woes and glories.

How to approach God; this is what we learn, its detailed technique through Narek?

Word 24, 3[7]

" Because I ate the lees of the bitterness my own deeds,
Being cooked in my grief, remorse, depressions,
Mental tortures, physical illness of all kind,
Suspicions, fears, confusions, hopelessness,
Shames, scandals- public and incontestable,
Escape , and a quest for refuge –
Refusal, and pursuit abiding,
Then- journeys long and aimless –
Which brought me to Your feet,
You, my escape and rescue,
My salvation and atonement,
And the last Harbor –
Lord Christ, eternal God,
Son of God-Creator of all,
Who rinse even deserts with abundant waters,
Taking care of thirsty,
In all, You are a lover of mankind,
Merciful and tender, always ready to help,
Always victorious in all,
Giver of a wholesome life without losses,
Unite me to Yourself,
To Your Divinity Ternary –
In one nature divine united in Spirit!
From Your all creatures I glorify You,
Expressing my thanksgivings

---

[7] Chapters of Narek are denoted as "Word" (W)

Forever and ever! Amen."

Holy Trinity; the Theology of Narek

"I Am Who Shall Be" – this is the exact translation of Genesis 26:3,[8] in which God the Father hints to the mankind His promise to redeem our race through His established sacrificial worship, first Abrahamic, then through a New Covenant of Jesus Christ- born as God, existing before eternity, being with Father and Spirit for eternity.

God is recognizable as much as He reveals Himself. And the definition of God depends on the subjective will of God, as He formulates who He is and how we can perceive Him.

The orthodox dogmatic teaching is about the correct definition of God's nature and entity in the scopes of revelations received by the selected few, whom we call *fathers of the church.*

Our perfection depends on our apprehension of God.

Narek presents the perfect dogmatic description of God as an ultimate source of good;

"One Father to one Son, honored by one Spirit, richest in goodness, absolutely exempt of evil- glorified with blessings, profoundly exulted" (W 77).[9]

---

[8] (אֶהְיֶה אֲשֶׁר אֶהְיֶה, *ehyeh ašer ehyeh* [ehˈje aˈʃer ehˈje]) , Genesis 26:3

[9] (Wxxx) *Word.*

His doctrinal confession St. Gregory describes as a greatest treasure granted to mankind, as a source of existence, the only true deity worthy of all worship.

That confession is presented by apostles and by the apostolic councils- Nicene and Chalcedonic, the dogmatic teaching of the Holy Trinity and Christ as God and Man with *two indivisible and unmixable natures.*

We present selected verses from Narek, which can summon the profession of the faith, according to apostolic councils;

"We believe in one God, who creates from nothing,
Calling to life from nothing,
Being a life-giving Will Himself,
The only almighty Name,
Through whom all was created,
Who with the Holy Spirit descended from Heaven, and He was a Man in the womb of the Virgin Mary (W77, 1),
We confess Jesus Christ to be a Man like us (W19), a Man without vice, and, meanwhile, a perfect God, who with the Holy Spirit is of the same essence with the Father – who is indivisible as one God of the Holy Trinity, in unbreakable Three Persons, as an indivisible nature of glory.

We confess the Holy Spirit of the verity, emanating from the Father eternally, and it is the essence of the entire existence (W14) ;

We bless and glorify the Father and Son, indivisibly pouring together with the Holy Spirit (W75), an eternal essence equal to Father, glorified with the Son. As Three Persons they are own identities, yet they are united in substance (W13, A).

And Christ had taken in His Body all blames with humble patience, and He was resurrected alive and self standing in the height of the Light – sustaining His perfect Body and perfect Deity (W75,4). Christ , who immaculately was born in the law of the spirit, which confirmed His Body , as the gold is confirmed in the fire, and as the light is confirmed in the air, never getting altered or getting separated from them (W34,5)- and He is glorified with the Father and the Holy Spirit, uniting our nature with His essence, a mystery, which can not be examined (W80).

We confess in right faith the Church of the Altar to be a divine dwelling place, which is as high as the Heaven, which is established on the order of twelve apostles and which is incensed by their disciples.

The Holy Altar of the Church had begun in the Last Supper Room, where the Holy Spirit had descended at the great Pentecost day (W75,7).

We believe in the Mother Church, which is fed on the milk of the Virgin Mother of God and presents Her Icon,   and   which   recreates   miraculously   and mysteriously through the redeeming art of the Holy Cross (W71, 12).

We believe through the worship of His crucifix the Verity of His Almighty Resurrection, His return in Glory for the Second time, for the severe Judgment,

We are bowing to the Holy Spirit, which will crown us with Christ to reign eternally (W73, 2, W52, 2).

Narek presents the expansion of this doctrine, rather reflecting it in all its details and richness of depth, as a pure lake, in which the bosom appears so near because of the crystalline pure water, that one can see all in a mere vision.

The Holy Trinity is the inner light for the author exposing his inside, and the mystery of God inwardly progressing.

Every human word of true confession and deep remorse, glorification and thanksgiving- breathes inside the Trinity, presenting a proof of Narek's loyalty and a true love for Christ, which reforms us too per se establishing our mind and soul in orthodox profession.

The more we go into it, the more we understand that the *true prayer is an inward bleeding process*.

A True Prayer as an Inward Bleeding Process.

Narek is a sincere word coming from the heart.

The state of the prayer is an ultimate sincerity and honesty of the soul, in which we present ourselves to God, and it is not an easy process, it is rather bleeding in pain .

If we succeed to follow Narek dwelling in its words, we will be capable of inner miraculous transformation, first by seeing our own image presented by Narek's confessions, than by seeing the direct miracles of God, for which this book through centuries was called *miraculous.*

It is not easy to dwell inwardly with the words of Narek, because it requires enormous efforts, a **concentration of mind and will** to keep up with the intensity of prayers. And when we do it, we see our own real picture face to face, the *way God sees us.*

Once we can see us from aside, we become *unconquerable*, we turn *free from the bondages of the mind*, we get filled with the *grace of the light-* as St. Gregory depicts it (W3).

Once we see us as God sees us, we turn into a new person. That is what Narek achieves .

Narek is penitential, a direction for our mind and heart, and once we take that direction, we get a nourishment for our feelings and mind, to discover our life in new meaning, making our mind to see and to recognize through our heart, which is now alert.

To see and to think by heart- this is a saintly category.

The spiritual power of the person is pending on the person's profession of faith and worship.

Our substance is a tantamount of our worship- it can be true and saintly if directed to Christ, the only true Trinitarian deity, or it can be false and imaginary, if directed to fallen demons, to which all the rest of religions serve, serving our sick ambitions in a first place.

The confession of sin and estrangement from a sin, in glorification and recognition of Christ ; that is what the perfection path is all about.

With almost supernatural vigor St. Gregory could crystallize all human feelings and thoughts, their effects and destructive inclinations. The saint brings together the border lines of life and death, eliminating the distance between them, and it is a high architectural ethics of Armenian ecclesiastical mind.

Armenian tomb stones are blossoming architecture curved on the stone, which we call "Khachkar"- cross-stone, and they denote the extirpated death and the victory of life.

The human tragedy in this Valley of Tears is under the blessing of Christ's resurrection, and it is a happy *tragedy* and a happy *death*.

It is in this oxymoron, where the human genius is being born, it is this oxymoron which procreates the human genius, *making human to be equal to God.*

In Armenian Christian culture they never post a statue of a diseased on the tomb, they post the flourishing crucifix, announcing the eternal spring and Paradise present on the consecrated ground for the blessed soul.

Cross Stone, IV A.D, Geghard, Armenia

What is the real tragedy for St. Gregory?
It is to know Christ and do not have Him, to live for truth and never reach its perfection.
The powerful voice of Christ is echoing in Narek, and it is a menace;

"Be you therefore ready also: for the Son of man cometh at an hour when you think not.[10]"

What a tricky God!

No this God is saintly. He means we should guard day and night our soul; our heart, mind, and body, to which our soul is depending. We should keep it for the Kingdom, do not wasting it, outwearing our life, as if our soul is disposable junk.

We are precious in all- that is what this call means.

We worship God in heart not in lips- and that is how we have to preserve ourselves for God.

We give birth to ourselves in penitential labor, for we are called to be new in Christ, adopted by God, immortal; and it is not an easy task.

We insult others, after which we suffer the exact pain we caused to others, and we suffer even much more, then we express our sympathy and compassion to those whom we offended- after which the forgiveness and love is being reestablished.

It is the same with God. Being God's own children with divine spirit, yet we debase that spirit, and with us we debase God, and it hurts Him so much. And when we understand and amend ourselves in sorrow- that is how we express our true love to our Creator.

And our real grief is when we, understanding the devastation of the damage, can not find a proper attitude for our mind and soul to expiate our sins;

---

[10] Luke 12:40

"To go to labor, and do not give birth,
To mourn, and yet be dry with no tears,
To be able of reasoning, yet do not sigh in guilt,
To thicken as clouds, yet not be able to shower a rain"
(W2, 2).

Narek describes the stony heart, incapable of sensitivity, as if it is a pebble under the water of a river; no matter how long and how much it is being inundated with water, always inside the pebble stays dry and rigid. That is how a human hardened heart is unresponsive to God's grace.

The person who has lost his ability to live others' pain as own, sharing others' pain and joy as own, who is no longer capable to give, to give in abundant and from heart- for this kind of person St. Gregory describes an appropriate status;

"He will ask- and will be unnoticed,
He will moan, and will not see a mercy,
He will offer sacrifices, yet will stay unclean,
He will see You, and will have no part in You " (W2, 2).

And what is reserved for a person like this?
It is a perfect death. And this death is not the corporeal death, which in fact is temporal- it is an eternal condemnation of the soul and body, when during the

second coming of Christ, this person will see Christ, and will see the Heaven overt – and he will crackle like a lighted candle, melting away, its lip light annihilated by the true Light of God (W2,2).

It is the perfect knowledge of the perfection of God, which makes St. Gregory to present us in perfect impurity, it is God's real presence in Narek's sacred space, in which we are afraid even to breathe, otherwise we would stain God with our breath; we in all are sordid.

St. Gregory weeps with the grief of one, who knows the pain of a loss; he weeps with the tears of Adam, and makes us to do so- opening our wounds, making them to bleed; to live a pain of a loss of the lost Paradise.

That is a lamentation under which the earth is shaking in awe.

Starting his work, St. Gregory asks God for guidance, in order the manuscript, which he undertook to write, be in accordance to God's will. Not only, he plans to achieve his own salvation through it, expecting as a reward for exposing all his unseen sins to receive abundant tears, which will shower his soul, washing it clean.

Amazingly this is true as well for all who read Narek, following it by heart, in which case the abundant tears really accompany the reader for the rest of the penitential life – achieving the greatest miracle of the recreation of the new person.

Narek is a reservation of a room in Kingdom, as St. Gregory expects to be granted, and it is the harvest of his sorrows – a complete redemption in Christ (W2, 2).

Starting from the Valley of Tears we end up in the Upper Glory of Heaven. Starting as man we end up as God in Christ.

Until then- the Book of Lamentation, the Book of Tragedy is ongoing, nonstop; from our first cry to our last gasp.

Amazingly in each prayer segment we see ourselves united to Christ as a final chapter, then every time with a new segment we return to our fallen place; the salvation labor is recurrent, and it is not done until it is done. This is a key of the orthodox worship, its highest ethics pleasing God, its divine nature and seal of nobility. Pride destroyed man, this humility elevates man.

The goal of Narek is clearly stated; "To expose human passions" in all their symptomatic expressions, with no mercy, with no reservation, to lash them ruthlessly, to cut their chains fettering a human down; to free human from carnal slavery.

If we see and know our passions we can uproot them as well (W3, 3).

To be healed from our passions, it is enough to be sorry, to be restored in our self- dignity, which is the faculty of our Creator, and our dignity of human is also His dignity as God.

Narek takes us some times too far in this inner journey inside our own souls, and very often there are so many questions which we have no answers for, and then- we *trust in God*, who even *from our weaknesses emanates the ultimate good.*

Without that trust our life would be like a summary of nonsense.

Every time we recognize in us a sin with a will to destroy it , we deliver a root down into a fertile soil as a tree of paradise, deeper and deeper, then this tree develops branches and foliage, then it flourishes and produces fruits. But **no. It is not possible without Christ.**

In reality even after our confession and repentance the tree is a monument to our vanity, unless this confession includes the sins of the *entire mankind,* sins of every fellow men, confession for any possible sin, which is human capable of, because every each of us has the *inclination* of all sins committed by men.

The tragedy of Narek, *from personal is developed to be universal,* in this way coming closer and united to the universal tragedy of all mankind. In this way we now, through Narek, face the universal evil, and the clash with it is unavoidable.

Or rather, there is no clash, if we don't serve the evil- there is only a victory, and it is the Victory of Christ. In this victory the cosmic evil does not have a power on us, we, who were baptized in His Name, under the protection of His Spirit.

We partake that victory only when we partake of the Sacrifice of Christ, which is for us to feel sorry for our own transgressions and live for others in good conscience. We share the Victory of Christ only through His Golgotha, when we share that trail, going through it, turning into martyrs of love.

And so- Narek is a holy martyrdom presenting a victim soul, through which we unite to Christ.

The Creator has created us in His glorious image and likeness, refilling our weakness as his opus with fullness of His love (W5, 1). The incarnation of the Logos, Reason, His Son, has a mystery to affiliate us and make us equal to Him, as His friends and kin. However, we lack a will in order to stay in the covenant, which God had sealed up with us, we as Israelites of later ages, scorn and break our contract up, turning our living soul to death and non-gods under the burden of sins (W5, 3).

We oath to wear Christ inside us not outside only, and those who don't do it, eventually face physical, mental, and spiritual ruins soon or later. The entire mankind, all equally have been impersonated in prodigal son, in adulteress woman, in the tax-collector, in the thief on the cross, etc...These are lucky ones who came to their senses at the end, compared with those, who persist and perish in their godlessness, by deafening and silencing their consciousness to the end. Even though the listed people might have been more fallen, yet they are saved in Christ, unlike those who being better, die without Christ and lose their souls for ever.

Even one of the killers of Christ, Paul, turned into an apostle of Christ- which is the greatest miracle itself (W11, 1).

Once "irrecoverable outlaws" they turned into blessed angel-like creatures in Christ; a thief on the cross turned into a judge of murderers, the dishonorable prostitute turned into a "mother of penitents" (W6, 1).

That is how the Lord elevates the human who is conscious about own weaknesses and misdeeds, knowing the nature of evil, neutralizing it with a hatred toward sin.

All, which is a human has to do is to get rid of self deceptions and imaginary worth described to himself, killing the phantom of own delusions about himself and the people around, about values of life, to leave all behind and follow Christ with own cross, toward the roads of thorns and hardship, the roads of self-analysis and self-inquest under the spiritual light of God.

It is painful to be stripped of delusional merits and a made-up dignity, to be presented to God as is.

To understand the terrestrial nature of human and to *restrict* that nature is a life lasting process, revamped in Christ at the end, if persisted in it (W6, 4).

Therefore, the repentance of Narek leads us to;

1. The acknowledgement of our own sins *in ratio with God's holiness,*

2. To obtain a *will* through the faith to be reconstructed in Christ.

We accomplish the first in deep and unceasing contrition and remorse, the second we do in humility and submission as a freewill final act of *"Your Will Be Done."*

Word 46

"a.I am an itinerant chastised and driven away ,

a wild creature upbraided by death,

keeping inside me   a herd of pigs, which can graze only,

a hireling in all,   never being true-

as it is in "Canticle," when it says;

I never knew who am I, in which image, and why I was born?

b. You, person my ignoble , were constructed on your two feet ,

always upright and erect , your head up to see all from above,

o you wretch! Now you are bent by your own will as a wild animal always in want ...

Where is your reason , which adorns you as a fire of the candle illuminating around?

The Reason, which is given to you in order to understand the temporal ,

Making sense of it,

To understand the lawful specimen and to see God."

The Reconstructive Staircase; Logos and Logos God.

As long we know the true God and we glorify Him, we will never lose our souls, or stay on the spot where we have fallen once, for the faith in Christ means *a process.*

"The ugliness of the entire mankind is in me" (W9,2)- declares Narek, hoping on the trimming hand of Christ, who would cultivate him in care and make him to be transformed; filled up with hope, when committed evil, filled with life, when dying a death, filled with Lord's grace, when finding himself in abomination, elevated to Heaven, when being low as reptilian, capable of humility in wild thrills, being meek, when caught by arrogance, locking for peace, when adversity prevails. All is in faith and in progress- when failure can turn into a success, and a success into a failure, if we don't humble ourselves to the Word of God, to Logos, to Reason, materializing our divine capacity to extradite our will to the syllabus of conscience.

Humbling is to reconcile. Humbling is to endure, to love, and hope.

This reconciliation serves God, who gives us a full credit for our temperance, keeping us under His mercy (W11, 2, 3, W12, 1). The virtues of love and hope are a result of our faith in Christ. It is through these virtues we can breathe in God as *spiritual beings* (W10).

St. Gregory is looking for reconciliation with God, and it can not be achieved even through his most severe penance, for there is nothing which might justify man before God- but it is possible only *through the incarnation mystery of Jesus.* Therefore, only the cognition of Jesus Christ's Person can produce the perfect reconciliation of God with man. It is through the Gospel and through the apostles we are in real association with God, and through the Church doctrine, which is the accumulation of God's wisdom , a reservoir for human civilization to move forward to eternity.

To respond to the call of Christ and to accept the holiness granted for free, is a main virtue of human;

"Seal Your Name upon my vision, keep Your Hand upon the structure of my body, anoint by Your Blood the entrance of my soul, and by Your crass lead me through exit, bless my peace and keep my bed immaculate – and You retain my miserable spirit" (W12, 3).

And the more we get grace, the more we are free of our sins, the more clearly we see them in us augmented as termites – never being capable of disengaging ourselves from the fetid low nature.

The more God gets closer to us, the more wholesome we enclose the sins of all mankind in us- from Adam to the last born.

"I have sinned against Your glory, and now- the blame on me is not coming from men, like it was the case with Job, but from You, Almighty- all seeing and all merciful, " (W 37, 1).

If I am not guilty in any sin against anybody, I am guilty against God's glory for the sins committed by others- for under this universe the mankind is one body, and it is united to the Body of Christ.

That Body is greatly reviled, and we are here to defend It.

When we humble ourselves, taking on us the sins of mankind, bringing ourselves low, we elevate God, and we act like Christ, who was killed as a criminal being the Only Just.

What God hates is the spot where we have fallen, what God pleases most is to see that spot abandoned and yet remembered by us throughout our life.

There is no person without sin in this world. And when we say we don't sin- we lie (W15, 4).

Jesus Christ only is without sin, He is a perfect Man and perfect God, and I am a perfect fallen human *capable of all sins humans commit-* and when we confess this, we find ourselves in the elevator taking us to Heaven.

A Dual Will, Bifurcate Human, Dichotomy of Person

When describing the resurrection of Lazarus, St. Gregory confirms that it is through the faith of Lazarus' sisters, Martha and Mary, through which the resurrection of the dead person occurred in God's will (W11,1).

The resurrection of Lazarus is averment for any of us, inspiring faith and hope.

But the saint depicts himself in a context of errant scenario as a split personality, who suffers his own weakest half, which sticks him to the constant deficiency.

"I have committed a spiritual suicide," (W21, 3) adding to it later, "I, who am not fully dead for this world, and not fully alive for God; I am not fully hot, or fully cold-" a lukewarm state, which is most hateful to God (W26, 1).

The reason of this inert spiritual state has been found also;

"When I observe the depth of the wastage of my thoughts and deeds- I find it immeasurable" (W26, 3).

Do not serve fully God, to have a dual will, to be connected to the transitory world by desires and dreams, chasing after futile worldly objectives- in fact, all this is a violation of the First Commandment, and anyone who belongs to the Church of Christ, to the

Kingdom, is a fig tree cursed by Christ, if single-mindedly does not pursue after the spiritual blessings of God, leaving all earthly behind.

The mental torture of St. Gregory is caused by this duality of will, by this double, twofold personality, serving in half God, in half self; so he is caught between the evil and good, between the virtue and sin, between the faith and apostasy – knowing both, and yet not being capable of observing a strict extraction.

The word of the Word, words of Christ should make us poor in spirit, and we can not use a saintly status to adorn ourselves, to look good and special, and if we don't stand beside the lowest of the low, then the words of Christ do not live in our hearts. That is how the false devotion is.

Poor in Spirit- is a perfection; to have nothing, to yearn for nothing but Christ.

We should show a will to allow God to proofread every our thought and action, following the direction of divine will only – or our life will be the summary of tragedies.

"I hold two cups in my hand with two contents,
I have two doors- athwart,
I see my face in double vision,
I see two idioms in my mouth,
I see two feelings in my heart- mutually exclusive;
I see all fewer under two suns- one effusing murk,
another effusing combustion"(W30, 2).

And when we try to reconcile the Good with Evil, we weave the web of death, which slowly takes over our mind and heart, failing our will, and then the essence of evil prevails, destroying the foundations of goodness and benevolence, based on God, forging instead the leaflets of flimsy truths of humanism.

The essence of goodness is directly opposite to the essence of evil, and the antagonism between them is indivertible, unless the evil is disrooted completely. And it is the sacred mission of the universal Church; to uphold the law of moral and of faith, defining the civil laws and ecclesiastical laws– based on the truth of God; a civil law, which ensures the freedom of the individual in security, and the ecclesiastical law, which ensures the divine doctrine exempt of humanism-heresies.

The antagonism between goodness and evil starts inside us and develops into a social request. And if we conquer this ongoing battle inside us serving the system of goodness and justice, our social life will be adjusted itself- assimilated into a City of God.

The Person of Jesus Christ is a model for the entire mankind.

Go back to the Gospel and observe His Person, observe Him in His saints and martyrs- the only heroes of human society, and after this it will not be possible to retrograde from this all-loving, all-self-sacrificing Hero!

The author of the Narek presents the pivot of this heroism; him taking on himself all iniquities of human race, assuaging the flagellation of *Ecce Homo.*

Woes and Mea Culpas

"WORD 21
A Word From the Depths of Heart to God

a. I have behaved myself as dead ,
Never being able to stand up like a man,
Never being able to receive a rational heart according to the Scripture-
And because I have never been better from my original fall,
Unable to move through the way of the goodness -
Here I will expose my dark inside
Do not sparing any evil feature
Narrated henceforth.

b. Alienated and evil as a plague - as I am-
I had confirmed the legions of Belier
Inviting them to dance , playing with cunning cheaters
With my lax and slack grants -
As a result of my secret deeds
With these ruthless butchers ,
 I am wounded mortally .
Those who were exiled by the Cross of Christ,
Had been invited back and empowered by me.

It is because my lawlessness
The Name of Christ is being insulted among nations ,
As it happened   when heathens insulted the same Name
Because of lawlessness of Israel .
Instead of being ruthless to the worms and rust,
Which had destroyed the garden of my soul,
According to the Lamentation of Joel,
Who had described Israel eaten by the same evil spirit-
I had collected these soldiers of the death
Inside me and against me,
Calling them to life
Against myself-
Always with them rising against Creator,
Always loyal more to destroyers than to Him.

c. Alas! Woe to me, who is wreaked !Grief, in danger!
A dark shame, as I am, with hidden blames.
And how I can dare to bring this all up?
My lamentations are too great- unbearable -
And if I could to see the picture of my soul,
How ugly and paralyzed it would be exposed -
Smeared with filth as a pagan temple,
For it is the same to serve the sickness of the sins ,
Or to serve the melted-shaped idols of madness!
That was the road I had chosen-
Turning the part of me, which You desired for Yourself,
Into a virginal desert of emptiness,

As You blamed the priests of Israel according to Your prophets .

How can I call myself a human, when I am in the list of inhuman?
How can I call myself rational, when I am fooled by my animal instincts?
How can I call myself visionary, when I had extinguished all lights inside me?
How can I declare myself a sensitive man, when I had lost my ability to feel?
How can I present myself an intact man, when I have now a dead soul?
I can not call myself even breathing or animated–
For I am no longer spiritual or rational –
As Jeremiah says - caught in the pain of Jerusalem -
I am in a trap of the death,
Abandoned for sighs and woes
For the rest of my life, as the psalmist says.

d. I do not hope on some creature,
As a cursed one by the prophets–
You, o Lover of souls!
You, Who on Your Crucifix
Were praying for your killers to the end
Asking for the greatest mercy
A charity in fullness for them–
Now grant me too the hope of your Redemption,
You, Life and Refuge!

In order before I breathe my misery out,
I could receive your Spirit of Goodness,
And to You, with Holy Spirit, and with Father on Highs -
Victory and Glory eternal. Amen. "

Knowing the perfect concept of God, being in baptismal grace and yet commit deeds, speak and think things which are contrary to the spirit of God- this is a great misery of human soul;

"Those who reached the justice of God and yet comply with injustice – deserve death" (W47, 3) .

And chain of woes and lamentations follow, every link of it connecting us to our own inferiority;

"You granted me to be alive, I returned to my death..
Woe to me !
I provoked the anger of my Creator...Woe to me!
I am incapable to gain back my peace.. Woe to me!
A fuel as I am for the fire of hell...Woe to me!
I weaved but the net of evil to my demise ...Woe to me! " (W7, 3).

Then St. Gregory with a genius inspiration starts to efface this cycle of *woes* with the galore cycle of *mea culpas.*

"Mea culpa! Against your Almighty beneficence- I am ignoble!

  Mea culpa! Against your unreachable gifts granted for free- I am eternally beholden!

Mea culpa! Against your adorable Body and Blood -for partaking them unworthily! " (W27, 2)

The tears from sincere heart are fertilizing showers for a soul to grow, and it is also a traditional ethics of prayer taught by our saintly fathers, as a *papal law*.

Saying *mea culpa* is the ultimate wisdom, which will take us to the upper levels of Heaven. And it is the reason why this segment of Narek is in Armenian canonical liturgy.

The principle of Narek *to arise through humbling myself is* the living and breathing Church, where our redemption is being achieved in Christ, and we are being sanctified.

It is after *Woes and Mea Culpas* when St.Gregory earns the visitation of Virgin Mary, an event, about which he mentions in Narek (W27, 3), and also- it is recorded in the act of St. Gregory.

St. Gregory Narekatsi was working on his book *Narek, The Book of Lamentation,* in the monastery of the island amidst Lake Van, Western Armenia, called "Ar Ter," translated as *"Take the Lord."*

One day, early in the morning, he was on his way to the church, when in the sudden illumination he met the Blessed Virgin Mary, with the Child Jesus on her arms.

The island was arid and covered with thorns. St. Gregory saw the Mother of God walking on thorny shrubs, and every time she stepped on the sharp thorns they turned into roses.

Then our Lady turned to St. Gregory, and by extending her hands holding the Child, she said to the holy monk;

-Gregory, Take The Lord For You!

And the shivering saint fell on his face; the Only Begotten is given to him for protection, and it is this poor monk's liability to safeguard the Child and His Mother, which he does in tears and penance until the end of his life.

St. Gregory was told to "Take the Lord"- now he, through his immortal prayerbook, tells us the same, to each of us; "Take the Lord for you!"

O how profound is St. Gregory's grief when he is speaking about himself, o how profound is St. Gregory's excitement and absolute happiness when he is glorifying God, exulting the greatness of the Queen of Heaven, the omnipotence of the King of Heaven.

The Virgin of Narek is an Immaculate Conception; we see a clear formulation of this dogma by St. Gregory in astonishing verbal eloquence, which is impossible to translate. The language of ancient Armenian, Grabar, in Narek sounds as a divine effusion; one can only dissolve in it.

Word 80, 1

"Now you see me broken in bitter grief,
Worthy of to be brought to naught-
Now prostrated in front of you, my Holy Lady, Mother of God,
I beg you to offer my plea, as if it is your own,
To your mighty Son.
You, Holy Mother of God, not a human, but a human-angel,
An immaculate cherub embodied,
The Queen of Heaven, unalloyed as air and pure as a light,
Without spot as a sun at the noon,
Immaculate above all sanctities created,
You are as a place, where there is only a promise and achievement,
Were there is only a paradise,
As a life-tree of immortality protected by the fire of the spirit,
Established and affirmed by the hand of God;
In your immaculate nature- you are so compassionate toward the fallen ones,
In your unspotted holiness – you are a patron and protector to such as I am,
Accept my supplications,
For I confess you as a Mother of God and of all,

For I trust in you, as you are the tree producing fruits of immortality,

As you have given birth to the Fruit of Immortality! "

Now we see through the eyes of St Gregory, now we know the power of the Mother.

We see also how paltry we are, daring to approach the divinity from our "harmful posture," seeing that divinity face to face as a revelation of God, as a *"Magisterial Creator-Writer"* and an *"Awe Inspiring Humility"* (W27, 3).

That is how God looks like; *awe inspiring humility.*

Look at me! I am a *terror inspiring pride* rather! Woe to me!

It is that Image of the *awe inspiring humility,* which makes St. Gregory to flay himself in spirit, to burn his personal all, to dissolve into self oblivion – contemplating only God in amazement, and in affright, in utter joy and in torment of self lynch – and it is a Hope witch is being breed as a result (in love and faith).

The definitive understanding and cognition of the good and evil, in their absolute forms- the neutralization of self-consistent evil in perfect act of will- only after this we see God and dwell in Him.

And then God paints in us His Image of Christ with His Light (W27, 4).

The Sacrifice Acceptable To God is A Pure Heart and A Humble Soul

The basis of the pagan religions is the cult of man, instead of the creator of a man.

The deity, which we choose to worship, can be false , in which case we will suffer the dire consequences of void inspirations , and if we observe the real nature of God through the reason, we can apprehend its composition, God as a pattern of life, where everything makes sense.

The central question of Christian religion is a reasonable comprehension of the true deity, a deity, which is present in our life, never interfering it. By the pattern of events, it is not difficult to notice that goodness generates goodness making one's heart joyful, and evil generates evil killing one's heart.

Goodness is of God. God has a nature of absolute goodness.

God was incarnated as a Man, as an Author of absolute goodness. This Man was not created, He is a Creator. Goodness is parallel to love and this incarnation is an ultimate revelation of God *as Love.*

When Christ had revealed Himself, the world was tired of pagan abominations, and the nations one after another accepted the God of Love, law and order-seeing in Him the meaning of life and death, connecting both as dots connected.

God once blessed the earthly tomb and pronounced, "This is your body!"- creating Adam (earth-man),

now the same God blessed the bread and wine and pronounced , "This is my Body and Blood!"- leaving Himself to us in the form of *substantial supernatural Bread.*

And all what Christ demands from His creatures is to be humble like Himself, understanding the limits of earthly nature and renewing that nature in Christ.

St. Gregory hates the hypocrisy in men, which is the main tool of manipulation to affix own individuality in fiction. When they think about us what we are not in reality, that is the state when we are actors but not true selves. How long we can act? Not too long.

"They think about me what I am not-" mourns the saint (W27, 3), following the unmasking of own vices and bareness of virtues;

corporeal passions,

a satisfaction of desires to the stupor,

a lack of true goodness,

empty hopes,

delusional dreams,

vanity,

inanity…

"Now as I am stripped off from all adornments, making myself willfully a lunatic- I can see my own self as is in my shame,

for I live in sanctity unholy,

I live in virginity as filthy,
I honor only by lips- my heart is cold and indifferent"
(W28, 2).
And once we pull all weeds out from our soul's field,
suddenly we turn into a good soil where the seeds of
real virtue can grow, for we satisfy the qualification of
humility as followers of Christ.
Passing through this purgatory, where even an
imperfect thought is being confessed as a realized
action, Narek creates our new soul where, "Your Image
can show in me (us)" (W40, 3).

Infinitely Close, Infinitely Faraway;
Our Creator is infinitely close to us when we hate sin
and confess them, and He is infinitely faraway from us
when we love sin and do not notice them, in which
case the tragedy of a person forms gradually and
devastates everything . The axiomatic truth is outside
us, which ensures the tragedy as;

Our arrogance is the destructive power of God's glory,
Our depression is a sign of our impiety ,
Our love toward luxury is a defeat of reason,
Our whining from difficulties is the breaking up from
God.
Our pride is a religion in Satan. Under the magnifying
reading glass St Gregory shows the very subtle
inclinations of our sinful nature ;
our love-hatred,

our cowardice- cover up- buffoonery ,

our hypocrisy – camouflage ,

our vainglory and craving after pioneering,

vindictiveness,

calumny as if it is a criticism,

a volatile will , never accomplishing which is right (W47, 1, 2).

Through this perfect deliberation Narek elevates himself to God, with him elevating us also.

This is the definition of the triumphing faith.

Narek the Heir of Heaven

Is the goal of Narek to show only the distortion of human soul and inferiority of his nature; *"I am the image of entire mankind-"* as he declares (W50, 3)?

On the contrary.

In fact St. Gregory's cardinal commission is to accentuate the mission of the human, for a man was created by the Creator out of nothing, just by the will of God;

1. To render a meaning to his eternal existence,
2. To see face to face his Creator (W46, 1)-

and this is possible only through the grace of God, permission, if man interposes efforts from his reason.

These efforts consist in inner regeneration, when we separate wheat from chaff, [11] when we separate in us

---

[11] Matthew 3:12

all acquired disorders, restoring our nature in God, restoring our image as God, united to God.

A man is a legatee of his Father God, he is a God's successor , inheriting all which belongs to God.

The notion of *sin* is a human distorted nature in disharmony with God, and when we varnish it, we gradually degenerate our nature making death eternal, instead of choosing a life eternal in God.

Word 67

"a. The Just Word of Christ-God condemns me even more than it condemns the satan,

for It has emerged in order to destroy the deeds of my fallen forefathers, restoring in me the image of my archetype ; Christ-

a God almighty in Whom I am dissolved most authentically into.

The satan was not given any grace,

meanwhile I got all;

I am in communion with life, the satan is damned to death,

Christ is being sacrificed continually for me, the satan was discarded right away,

I am empowered by the crucifix , the satan is destroyed by it,

I am united to the founding Light, the satan was deprived of it,

I am given the Heaven even living on earth, the satan has no place even at the least,
I am in hope, he is in despair,
I am crowned, he is locked in a swine herd,
I bear Christ's Name, he is lowered to reptilian.

c. All I need is to be healed in You, my Nurse and my Bliss,
for You pity , You medicate ,
You recreate ,
You are unsearchable in Your power and might-
And I glorify You,
In Your genuine union with God, Your Father –
For ever and ever. Amen."

God is a prefect Love and Freedom, and He created a human as such, giving the human a free will even to choose the evil, and even to commit the most evil deeds, for human is stupid . This stupidity is cured by the Son of Man and God, and as it is in the mirror reflected- we all see our perfect self in Christ.
The definition of God is;
God is a perfect Love (1John:4),
God is an uncreated Light(1John, 1),
God is a righteous Judge (Psalm 7:11) .

God has created man for honor and glory ;
God has given to man His own Image (Genesis, 1),
God has given to man a reason and a genius creativity,

God has given to man an unbending tongue ,
God has given to man an angelic soul,
God has given to man a head with halos .

"You were given to cooperate with the Right Hand of
Almighty God,
being from the same breed , from the same species –
You were called to be a God, o my soul! "(W 46,2);

How awfully is presented the calling of human by
Narek, as a most profound and tremendous truth!
 Bankrupted from all divine merits, a human has
lowered himself to the animal genus – emptying
himself from his spiritual values, by losing his capacity
to stand above his human nature, to be supernatural.
Sensuality versus spirituality; this is a choice of men,
and it is a declaration of war against God, for man is a
supernatural creature , if he stays in God's grace, loyal
to his calling as a heir .
If this conspiracy against God has turned into a norm
upon which the human civilization is built, then who
will   be   saved   and   redeemed   deserving   the
rehabilitation ?
Who is the heir of God among mortals (W 31,3)?
The answer is *whoever is loyal to the history of
redemption,*   the   traditional   institution,   which
accomplishes the regeneration of the mankind, which
is the apostolic church and its seven sacraments.
Through the Christian civilization, its moral-ethical,

philosophical , cultural, and civil norms- the mankind has created the set of values , which lead the mankind to its sublime calling , to its perfection , to the grace of God, if the seven sacraments are used as a personal will.

Whoever possesses the Christian traditional heritage has also God's supernatural eternal heritage promised in full.

We forgive those who is guilty against us 7 X 77[12] (the numbers of infinity) – the same way our loving Father God does to us by infinitely forgiving our human weakness , if we love His nature, which is holy.

The lawless mob has crucified the just and innocent Christ. And how this is a justice?   The God's jurisdiction does not supply justice?

Rather – *the love of God is above own jurisdiction and justice* . Christ could have avoided the gruesome death He did not deserve, but He chose for Himself the death on the cross, or else- how could I know about His infinite love toward me? How could I understand that there are two places in existence – the place of those whoever kill the innocents and justice, called Hell, and the place of those, wherever are being innocent and just, standing to the end with Christ, called Paradise.

I have these to places to choose from; Dishonor or Honor, Inglorious or Glorious, Incomplete or Complete, be a human as my own, or a Human as

---

[12] Mathew 18-21

Christ's own, to be in death, according to decay, or in eternity, according to redemption…

I was damned by the inheritance of my fallen nature, I am elevated and restored by the inheritance of Christ the Savior . The ransom is paid. I am free.

"6. And the Lord said to me in the days of king Josias: Hast thou seen what rebellious Israel hash done? She hath gone out of herself upon every high mountain, and under every green tree, and hath played the harlot there.

7. And when she had done all these things, I said: 'Return to me, and she did not return.'"

JEREMIAS - Chapter 3

God has given to mankind a law, which tells us about divine will how God desires to see us, making us to take a U turn from our asquint ways.

Knowing the will of God yet a human is too weak to persist in pleasing God.

St. Gregory is horrified when bringing the example of King Solomon (W48).

Once being a beloved son of God, Solomon afterward was hated by God for his treason.

Once a trusted friend, whom God granted His most sacred secrets- Solomon turned into a deserter.

Once being a cause of peace and prosperity for his people, Solomon turned into a cause of mutiny and doom.

Once being a law of life, he turned into a damnation to death. Solomon abnegated his holy faith.

And if this was the end of this wisest divine men, what would happen to us?

How horrible is the sterility of Solomon's soul!

In the book of Ecclesiastes all is vanity and nonsense for Solomon ; he is barren and lost, the life was an emptied cup thrown away.

Life has no value; how Solomon could reach this point?

"2. Vanity of vanities, said Ecclesiastes, vanity of vanities, and all is vanity 16 I have spoken in my heart, saying: Behold, I am become great, and have gone beyond all in wisdom, that were before me in Jerusalem: and my mind hath contemplated many things wisely, and I have learned."

ECCLESIASTES - Chapter 1

Looks like the divine gift of wisdom Solomon has lost in his unconcerned and luxurious life, and his throne was in fact the trap of death.

Now empty-handed Solomon's last testament is in the formula; " Fear God and keep His commandments " (Ecclesiastes, 12).

Narek does not support this .

Narek is about the son's love toward his Father, pleasing Father rather in love than in fear, as we please the person when we love, ready to do all, which our beloved would desire.

"When I please Your will, even the darkness turned into a shiny ray for me" (W65,3).

The love for God in St. Gregory's heart exceeds the fear. And if we see the presence of that fear, it is only the fear of losing God, as a consequence of sin. St. Gregory fears to insult God's spirit and to upset Him, and this fear is not because of the due penalty only.

Using the example of Solomon, St. Gregory develops a system through which one can be exempt of fear and punishment of God , through which one can avoid to serve the evil, to be alert, *and it is when we understand the roots of evil;*

1. The lust for women and sexual pleasure through the worship of a woman, which can be a cause of every man's destruction.

2. The lust for glory, which empties a man from his wisdom, abating the senses ; all talents and graces given to a man should be directed to recognition and glorification of God, not for own notability, or he will be destroying himself.

3. Arrogance, which is the consequence of every power, be it from a social dominance, or wealthy status , or physical power .

St. Gregory remarks that the human weakness and perfection was not only typical to Solomon , but also to all chosen souls of God, like Moses, David, St. Peter, and that we all err "not being able to be saved on our own, if we do not trust completely in God" (W70).

Highlighting the weaknesses of God's elite, St. Gregory does not have intention to debase them, those through whom we can approach God"- on the contrary, his intention is to show the love of God for His human fellows.

St. Gregory confirms that "a human is capable of perfection, as much as he seeks after it " (W71,1). However, in every human being there is an inclination toward sin, for our nature is tainted – and every human is "a perfect image of entire mankind." And how we can dare to ask from God a punishment for sinners, if we are the first sinner among all?

How can we ask God, praying, "Give them according to their deeds" (W60,1), if it would be our own condemnation in a first place?

Even though very often our will is united to evil, St. Gregory outlines our main merit, which is a credit to sanctity ; that we elevate the Holy Spirit in us when **we hate sin.**

Our good will consists in hating sin and inclining to do good, and if we fail, no matter, God is there to fasten us to our good will again and again .

Our weakness is unwilling, our good will is inbred. And if we make our will to serve the will of God, all our weaknesses miraculously transform into a spiritual vigor.

The proof of the good will of mankind are the laws of Moses , the books of prophets, the epistles of apostles , the Gospel of our Lord, the witness of saints and martyrs (W64,2). All this together is the baptismal seal of the citizens of eternity in Christ's Name, and there is no other way for a man to be restored to God.

The Dogmatic Teaching of Hell According to Narek

Narek is experience, it is an accomplished journey through the purgatory and hell, for the purpose of it is to identify every sin in human soul and bring it up, to understand its effect, which is *hell*.

The sin disclosed is the Hell.

No one can avoid of death, and that fact should prompt us to ponder more often about death; what is it, how it looks like, are we ready to face it?

Hell is a place where sin lovers go, a place where there is no hope, no prayer , no end of anxiety or time, or a door through which it would be possible to escape (W67, 2).

Hell is where there is no God.

Narek confirms the *faith and remorse* as life-giving factors, in which case we are ready to face the judgment of God, meanwhile in the absence of these men are confused, terrorized , lost ...

The hell is a pain of losses , and it is eternal .

"The sky turns material,
and the earth waves like a sea and collapses,
the foundations of universe and sky shake,
the mountains turn flat, the substance of nature melts
in fire .
And then the Heaven is being opened as is, and all
creatures are shown in their inner gist.

"The hidden deeds will be shown,
our secret thoughts and passions will be outlined,
our paths and procedures will be visible to all,
our emotions and feeling will be sealed on our bodies
to characterize us –
then all eyes will see the Lord and His awful Advisory
Board " (W79, 3).

St. Gregory depicts the indescribable horror of man
when he is facing God.
This vision of Narek's Hell does not inspire
hopelessness, for St. Gregory's purpose is to lead us
through our inner darkness to the Light of Christ – and
that vision, as a manifestation of self-condemnation,
finds a grace from God, and it turns into a bail of
salvation.

Word 79

"As if I escape from a lion,
meanwhile I face a bear,
As if I escape from a bear-
Finally reaching home and closing the door behind,
Then suddenly the snake falls upon me from a ceiling.

There is the ark of principal convicts,
There is the gospel of Gospel killers,
Through the Cross, the Eucharist, the Holy Blood,
And the Holy Altar –invisibly present-
There will be an eternal scene opened to condemned;
The dungeon, in a form of the beast –
In which I will recognize all my fabrications …"

Jesus Christ; The Mystery of Eucharist

Narek is a summary of life, a life spent in isolation, penance, self-mortification, prayers, and fast, a life spent in holiness. It is a recapitulation of our human life's worth and an abrogation of a natural death.
Through this theology we are exempt of pharisaical worship of outer false unction.

"What is the benefit of being pure, if I will be tried as a pharisee and hypocrite, or where is the damage of my transgressions, if I will be praised like a tax collector? " (W50,1).

The true works of atonement St Gregory presents as following ;

    1. Without Christ there is no salvation of soul (W40, 3, 43), for –

"To know You is already to be perfectly just, to know Your power is a root of eternity" (W48, 1).

    2. Without the confession of hidden sins and without self-scourging there is no atonement (W50, 1).

It has been six thousand years since the creation of Adam, and the cognizant mankind expresses its gratitude to God through praise. The mankind offers its love to the Creator giving to God its best ; all just people from Abel to Christians offer the acceptable sacrifice to God, as God pleased . That is why God established the priesthood to do this job, and eternal Priest, Christ came to save mankind, offering Himself to God since unceasingly , for our sins are unceasing.

The ultimate expression of human reason is its capability to glorify God. But before doing it the mankind should verify if the deity glorified is a true one. The true deity is a source of Goodness without stain of sin or shadow of error, and Christ is presenting the true deity, the fulfillment of the teaching and divine promises. The alpha and omega – the perfect formula of a true deity is the Holy Trinity.

St. Gregory indicates that all creatures can witness the greatness of God, who has created the universe , sea-oceans, mountains, stars, human souls, angels- yet mankind is often stupid enough to worship the creation, nature, or own delusions, neglecting the true revelations of God.

In fact, God can not change a person by showing to humans the glory of His creation. Only through the *personal relationship with a person* God can transform a person in strict consideration of the person's free will, and that personal relationship is possible only through Jesus Christ.

All efforts of spiritual works are in vain, unless one finds his salvation in the Holy Eucharist , the Sacrifice of God to God, by uniting himself to that sacrifice in love.

By His own will Christ underwent through the supernatural sufferings of Golgotha ; this is a divine mystery through which those who participate that sacrifice are saved and are exempt of death (W53,2,47,3).

No one can be in God unless one understands the mystery of sacrifice, a covenant made between God and Abel, renewed with Noah and Abraham, according which the sacrificial lam, the offering of bread and wine are replaced with Christ at the end of times, as it was promised through prophets .

Word 53,3

"You have turned into an unparallel pontiff ,
and has destroyed the old covenant ,

instead of animal sacrifice offering Your blessed Body ,
distributing It without a loss to all-
from simple sinners to hopeless convicts .
God of all, You have taken my image and my nature
to redeem me , as if I am embodied in You ,
United to You, bearing Your substance –
Meanwhile You has taken my place
presenting my vile self, taking the death I was under
to Yourself –
Dying many times , yet You are alive
in the Sacrifice offered by those who confess You as
God.
I believe in It, through It to obtain the life eternal -
Not by my merits, or even by my martyrdom,
but through the Life-giving Remedy of Your Sacrifice
the salvation is fulfilled. "

"You are a bliss, and it is my only desire: to die, in
order to have You." (W90,2)
"The Blood of Almighty is given to communicants,
which joy is overwhelming, and the sadness of Abel's
murder is no more " (W75, 7).
"I beg You, let me be worthy of Your heavenly
Remedy of Life, have mercy on me, for I am smitten in
soul and in heart" (W53,5).

St. Gregory exults the church calling her "mother,"
"breathing body," "a stage of trial," "ark of purgatory-"
which is alive through the Body and Blood of Christ.

Our Mother Church nurses us with the Blood of Christ, which is our maternal milk (W77, 12).

The Savior is our only hope , and the heavenly "Cup Full of Blood" is the remedy of our resurrection and eternal life. And there is no other (W95,3).

The climax of the Narek 's wisdom is;

-there is no condemned, for God can turn one from convict to free,

-there is no saint either, for God can condemn anyone through His scrupulous and just examination (W53,1).

Therefore, the *justification of a man depends solely on God.*

Man is not absolute evil, and he can dissolve into the absolute love of Christ.

The glory of God is in His absolute mercy, and we are called to be like Him, by loving God, by loving fellow men, by loving our enemies, as Christ does.

The law of Moses is about fear and punishment, the law of Christ is about love, confession, and penance, through which we reestablish our connection with God.

"You are not restricted in law, You are above the law, and You save when we confess You,

for You are the only law of the promised bliss for all sinners" (W53 5).

"I do call You not only the son of David, but also an incarnation of God's essence , confessing You as the Lord of the earth and heaven" (W17,2).

Man is hurt by sin, his conscious is darkened , for;

"the gored can not beg from You, for he was speechless, could not stare at You, for he was guilty , could not ask for mercy, for he was abandoned -"

a fallen man could not understand the mercy of God, let alone to call Him *Father* . That is why "foolishly man turned into a rebel and had cooperated with enemies' army against God" (W14,2) . It is because of this foolishness man put his hand on God and crucified Christ.

Christ is patient and not vindictive toward even His killers. He did not revenge, He even took care of them. He did not follow the law of Aaron to curse in return , to destroy in return, instead He pretended to be "pagan" and unaware of "tit for tat," unresponsive to written rolls and codes – following only the law of Love, which His nature provides (W14, 3).

The price of the God's Blood poured unjustly is the key for man to understand own evil and the mercy of God.

Here is the entire mankind, which is like a gored Samaritan injured from bandits, whom Christ took care of and saved (W14,3).

In this mystery of God's love, incarnation, sacrifice, and transubstantiation- His actual presence in ritualistic worship of the Eucharist - through this mystery we have the "greatest gift to be ourselves God" (W52,2).

Man has in himself the essential nature of God to be God; love , which is the pearl of creation put inside us, which can turn us as much perfect as God is, through God's grace in Christ.

Again, it is Narek's **dogma**; that man is not absolute evil , for the fallen nature of man has in it also the pearl of his Creator, that is why the betrayal of man can contain a particle of doubt, the arrogance can contain meekness , and even in ruse there can be a frankness- all this lead to hopelessness , which leads to penance , and even in enmity one can look for peace, even in war one can be in good-will, in death- longing for life (W31, 3).

"If I am a man- I am maniacal ,
 if I am a child- I am a prone to evil,
if I am rational- I am beast-looking ,
for I am in body,
troubled , causing a trouble too " (W22).

This is how man is imperfect in his merits . Therefore the true nature of human Narek dogmatizes as *"unstable existence,"* rather evil (W5,1), *and the stability of that nature is rather depends on the cognition of evil and good , when we distinguish and separate in us the evil from good,* putting evil in quarantine and deleting them gradually, like they are computer viruses.

St. Gregory Narekatsi is not a humanist, presenting a false understanding and false charity toward men, because he himself is presented as this universal mankind impersonated- seeing all his vices and merits under the perfect light of God.

Man is under the focus not of the human love but divine, therefore this humanism is divinely recycled and turned into a true vision of human value as eternal, humanity elevated to God, meanwhile humanism debases God to human, equally depreciating human and God.

No one can glorify the Holy Trinity and be accepted by God, unless one understands Its essence by understanding the "essence of the Holy Scripture , "after being *illuminated by the light of a true faith* (W 62,2).

That is why every chapter of Narek explains the nature of Trinity, the basic doctrines, as they are dogmatic signatures of God- following the glorification of God united to psalmist.

Narek's Divine Signatures

Narek's profound rational reaches the essence of **"inaccessible space of God,"** touching it as **"unceasingly adjacent "** (W23,1). Thanks to this intimacy St. Narekatsi is granted the taste of the Lord and the grace of sanctity, which is given for free.

The God's grace is sealed in every page of Narek, communicating us as well, if we read Narek from depths of our souls- as it is intended for.

Our souls communicate Narek, and we recognize ourselves, and we recognize God , and we turn into children of God, through;

suffering the pain, which human causes to God because of his sins,

suffering the pain, which sin causes to us by distorting our divine image ,

suffering the pain – be it friend's or enemy's- by mourning their condemnation and foolishness, when they are away from God,

begging and offering sacrifices in fast, charity works, in prayers, for the lost mankind is rejecting Christ, its Savior.

This is how we are being adopted by Christ – for our universal mission to participate the redemption process of humanity.

St Gregory addresses to God as the "Foster Father of those who suffer, and are sensitive to share God's concerns, not only own." And this **unceasingly adjacent** God is owned by a person, when he is living the pain of all mankind, in spiritual vision seeing its status .

We are sons of God as much as we are able *"to sorrow according to God,"* and it is possible only when we intercommunicate with the suffering of Christ, His Passion Week, during which the evil of mankind had been revealed, as each and every one of us has a partnership with them who were whipping Christ, when they were crucifying Him- and each of every one of us tortures Christ with our personal sins. That is why we always should be among the humble, most guilty , always kneeling in front of God , asking for His action to restore our human dignity , the honor of our human image, which is possible only *when we detest sin* (W50,1,2).

Christ is a declaration of Father's love toward the human race, realizing **a human as a spiritual creature, not material-** therefore as a heir not only of material and natural creation, but also of supernatural and spiritual.

St. Gregory perfectly confirms, that the human passes the test before God when he practices his virtue of forgiveness ; **forgiving those who are guilty against us is a greater supernatural achievement, and it is a divine inspiration possible only through Christ.**

After presenting all possible human sins in his person, St. Gregory reserves the right also to ask for entire mankind, for the salvation of those who confess Christ as God, and even for those, who are the enemies of Christians, for he presents also the vices of his enemies in himself.

"Do not destroy those who sting me, but only correct them -" for , as it is done by Christ too- when we ask for those who hate us, wishing them salvation, only then we are like God (W83,1,3).

"It is even more pleasing to God when we ask grace for our enemies , than for our friends " (W83,3).

As we see – if the Gospel of our Lord presents a path , Narek presents the realization of that path, the anatomy of human soul, who makes us to live the Gospel as life.

"Reward me, o Lord, for my bitter mourning and woes, by forgiving all , showing mercy to all, o King exulted, foster especially those, who are lost in most grave crime and hopelessness , and who die sudden and not being ready to die!
Please, consider me as just for saying this prayer! " (W36,1).

Word 83

"a. A Most High, Awful Power,
Not a subject to examination,
The Lord of creatures and the King of Heaven,
The source of Reason,
The Fire-Gate of immense blessings ,
The criteria of generosity , who never is vindictive –
Through this manuscript of human tragedy,
Which presents the confession of all sins of entire mankind –
Consider, o Lord, my supplications and look at us in mercy ,
Consider us to be good ,
For Your love sake toward me in Christ's Name,
Be merciful also to our enemies,

Neglecting their meanness, their guilt,

For, they might be right when they ill speak about us,
Christians,

For if I bring forward what is really inside me,

I may be even less worthy of Your love and mercy
than them.

c. I pile my empty days, which are useless and void, as
it is my life,

for I am useless from the day I was born,

but , please, Almighty, do not thrash me,

as You did it to the house of Judah and to the
generation of Ephraim.

Instead of good seeds I cultivated the poisonous weeds
in my soul,

which anaestetized me , dulling my senses ,

in the end turning into curses and thorns of sins-

I did not disseminate justice ,

I reaped the curse as a harvest ,

and not the fruits of life, according to Osee.

the breast of my virginity is dangling –

I lost my innocence, as the prophets say about Israel.

But, You, o Lord, can restore all –

Even if I present the devils, which used to live in
Judas-

You can make me sober and clean .

If You could make a virgin out of prostitute–

How much I would be blessed when I conjoin You,

O Lord, if You please!

Most terrible quagmire You can dry in one instance,

The same way You can clean my soul from its inner pus.

d. Accept those as just, who looking at my clerical robe take me for a saint and prophet,
meanwhile there is nothing is hidden from Your eyes, and You know who really I am –
justify them, as they accept me in Your Name, as if I am a depository of Your relics.
They think about me that I am blessed,
 just by looking the beauty of my vestments and glory – meanwhile I am wretched in all .
Purify me, as they think about me, and accept them in reconciliation –
Granting them the wreath of salvation –
From Your immeasurable mercy and love."

The Church; The Only Device of Mankind's Salvation

All true Christians know the power of the Holy Cross. And it is wrong to call Christians Cross-worshipers, for we worship not the cross, but the Blood of Christ poured upon the cross.

That Holy Blood is giving the power to the cross, and when the priest blesses it, it turns into a sacramental, into a holy object acceptable to God, and blessed by God with a supernatural power.

The physical construction of the church starts from that cross, which is at the top of the dome as a key element of the church's architecture.

The Holy Cross is the horror of the demons. Especially the ritualistic passions of Christ in unbloody sacrifice, offered on the holy altar, at the holy mass.

The hell is destroyed through the cross and through the sacrifice of Christ .

The apostolic church from the top to bottom operates through that cross, and through the power of that cross the mass has a sanctifying effect for us.

The cross is a monument of death and resurrection, when we have it in our tombs —and whatever is unthinkable turns to be a reality; our eternal existence in the resurrection of Christ.

The Last Unction is a sacrament of exalting death (W90, 3). Once we seal our senses, body, heart, and soul with the cross- we preserve ourselves in the resurrection of Christ, ejecting all demonic powers .

That seal transforms all which is material and bodily to a supernatural and spiritual, that is why St. Gregory asks God to keep the cross on his breath and body to the end (W84, 2).

The crucifixion of Christ is a New Genesis Book, where in every mystery of the Christ's passions we are created in perfection, anew, as a new creature;

with crown of thorns, Christ has eliminated the sprout of sins, with the scourging, Christ has eliminated the pain of agony and death,

with the blasphemy of being spitted upon, Christ has eliminated our mental torture of shame (W60, 3).

The Crucifixion of Christ has terminated "the great dragon, the old Serpent , which betrayed the universe," overthrowing and killing the satan completely (W90,5).

Narek is exulting also the bell of the church under the crucifix.

The ringing bell of the church and its crucifix chases away all demonic itinerant powers around the church, keeping the terrain blessed and imperturbable (W90, 2).

Our communication with the Holy Cross , with the Passions of Christ , justifies us according to our faith , because the sufferings of the Only-Begotten can not be void (W78, 2).

St. Gregory asks the Lord "to plough the field of his rational-" asking in a first place to keep in grace the Catholic Holy Church, which he serves as a monk and bishop, and without which he can not teach Christ's divine doctrine of Miracle-Science. Only through the sponsorship of the mother church, with burning tears, with words of remorse and deeds of penance – he can approach the mysteries of Christ in order to taste the Lord (W34, 3).

The priesthood of the church has an obligation to pray everlastingly, to sacrifice day and night, in order through these acceptable efforts to save the flock of Christ at this "earthily Jerusalem," which will transform into Jerusalem of Highest with the Second Coming of Christ, living as His right-side's angelic class (W34, 4,5) .

The teaching of the Catholic church is apostolic, confirmed by the revelations of God, which means it is not made by human, but it is a divine inspiration.

Each and every sacrament of the church is a divine institution, and it is endowed with supernatural power performing miracles (to transform mortal man into immortal).

"Starting from the Last Supper the gift of God was achieved at Pentecost, through which we turn into children of light" (W75, 7). And if our service to the holy altar is not perfect, and we are not living members of Christ's Body- at the judgment our impurity will testify against us , because we have been communicating the Christ's Body and Blood unworthily (W79, 3) .

The Church is standing upright on the spiritual heritage of its heroes; martyrs, confessors, doctors, hermits, saints.

For every Christian the Church is a family, much closer than a biological one.

St. Gregory loves the saints of the Church, and he depicts them as an ark of Holy Spirit, decorated with all heroic features, which a human can have; they are the elite of God. They are totally honest , they are totally just , sublime and brilliant , they are simple, with an open face and a direct glance , with innocent conduct , with a high character , stable and firm, sober and serous, they are always generous, their confession is unitary and consistent, steady , they have a courage which always wins even to the death, their vision is profound, without confusion, their virtue is divine, their words and actions are true, their image is immaculate and whole (W61,1). They are so perfect and so exemplary for the human race that "this world is not worthy to have even a single one of them" (W78,2). And they are so loved by God, that God allowed us to ask for their solicitation to obtain mercy for us; that is why we pray in their names too (W71,1). The Church is fixed on Christ and His saints, and no one can change an iota from canonized rituals and dogmatic teaching- or the heresy and evil will prevail. Narek is a holy pillar supporting the sanctity of the Church institution in its apostolic virginity. And this edifice can not be disintegrated.

The Veneration of The Holy Virgin Mary

As all doctors of the Church, the same way St. Gregory Narekatsi teaches us that the most effective way to communicate God is through Mother of God, Blessed Virgin Mary. We can not do it, unless we know fully the nature of the Mother of God, her great image as a first perfect creature, as immaculate conception, and as a first fruit of Christ's redemption, resurrected in body. We will summarize the dogmatic, divine description of the Mother of God, repeating the teaching of Narek.

We venerate Blessed Virgin Mary in the most glorious way, for she is the **Queen of Heaven**, for she is the Virgin **Mother of God** personifying the whole beauty of the Holy Spirit;

"Pure light,
Breathing Eden,
Precious treasure,
Holiness without trace of shadow,
Sublime testament,
The medicine of life,
Human-angel,
Immaculate cherub in body "(W80).

"The Tree of Life immortal , purged in burning light, empowered by the Father, patronized by God Almighty" (W80,1)- whose prayers are acceptable to God, for she is a maidservant of God in perfect meekness. She is the Bride of the deity, which has no beginning, elevated by God, chosen and purified from her conception at the womb of her mother. She is decorated by the Reason of her Son-condensing in her the greatest sanctity, which is equal to creative power of God; the maternity. And she is a mother to all elected mankind, and the nature of sin is entirely strange to her, and she is a crusader, bearing the cross of her Son – glorifying God in perfect union, making it possible for us to be united to God through her, our mother and caregiver, who is also a Queen of Cherubs.

The agony is the same moment, as it is the moment of our birth. St. Gregory calls for the Mother, who can make the birth process painless, turning the death moment into a happy blessing of rebirth and resurrection in Christ (W80).

The Virgin Mary is a perfect Mother because of the perfection of her Son. We pass from this world to the other through the bosom of God's Mother, who awaits us, as a midwife awaits for the coming of the baby, to help and declare the new birth, as our Mother admits us in Heaven, declaring our new genesis in eternal life.

To Triumph With Virtues; The Summary of Narek

"All I have is abominable thirty-silver pieces, which can not be stored in the treasury of the Lord " (W26, 2); this poverty of Narek's spirit lives in truth and triumphs through centuries.

St. Gregory Narekatsi makes us to live the sting of his remorse, and through Narek we live on earth our purgatory, if we read this prayer book with the sincere heart and simplicity. We emerge from the flames of this purgatory "as a new wine for the new skins" (Mathew 9:12).

The rational of Narek triumphs, when it declares, "You all our sins had considered as Yours "(W63, 3), declaring the humility of Christ in total self-denial, and in equal vigor St. Gregory declares his own humility and self-denial , "I am a bearer of all sins of all mankind" (W72, 2)- rescuing the name of humanity , regaining honor for all;

Word 65
"a. I am the patriarch of iniquity,
the principal of all outlaws ,
the first born of all condemned ,
the stereotype of felons –
here I narrated all which should be kept secret,
I made bare all my thoughts and deeds,
Vomiting the gall of my bitterness –
Betraying my plot and operation with evil,
Squeezing the pus from my wounds,
Showing the word of my vices,
Tearing up the mask of my hypocrisies ,
Exposed my ugliness,
Depriving my nakedness with covering rags,
Making my putrescent deeds to stink ,
I vomited with them the settling of death ,
I opened the metastasis of my inner cancer
To my Supreme Pontiff Christ.
I did not spare my ego,
I did not spoil my body by taking care of it,
I did not spare the roots of my old self-

And I was cruel to my very nature,
To its needs and whims –
Cutting all ties with them,
Destroying the cozy corporal castle,
Forging the will, making it to fight for its life-
In all way I annihilated the alliance with the deceiver -
But the outcome of this battle depends on you, O Lord
Christ! "

 His powerful and intense prayers St Gregory often
depicts as a "silence of heart-" and it has a profound
meaning; what sounds in words to us, to God it sounds
as a silent composure of penitent, waiting for his
sentence in humility.

Through the Narek' self burning confession St.
Gregory depicts "efforts of his will **against own
nature**"(W57, 2) . He confirms, that when we work
against our will and ambitions to expose our true
essence, our inner structure- exempt of decoration and
hypocrisy- only then we are adopted by God as His
children, standing above our human nature to be
supernatural.

In Love of Christ the greatest miracle is achieved; we
are comforted when we are in despair, we are indulged
in punishment, we are granted freedom in curse, we
are restored to life in death (W53, 2).

Truly, St. Gregory never reserves any merit to himself.
His soul is flooding with huge waves bringing up only
the filth and litter, which hides in depths of his nature,

and by his rational he makes this dissection declaring – " I am an animal " (W50, 2).

It seems too much; this self humiliation and self-annihilation, this process of dishonor and debasement. God is longing after us, as the Baby Jesus, who was born in the animal manger, is looking to live in our hearts, even though we, sinners, are unworthy of it.

At this point we, the average people, can not understand this great mystic, who had passed through a great mystery, and this experience can not be shared with him; St. Gregory saw God face to face in apparition, he , as it had happen to St Anthony, had the Baby Jesus in his arms, he met Blessed Virgin Mary one time when he was going early in the morning to the church for the service, as it is written in saint's act.

In fact our nature is not low at all, it is our mind and will, which surrenders.

St. Gregory presents a human as a low creature only in comparison with that encounter, when he saw face to face Christ and Blessed Virgin Mary.

When we face God, we find ourselves in the shoes of St. Peter, denying God so often, and not even noticing it- always finding ourselves so distant from God and so imperfect in all our endowers – with darkened memory and understanding of God and His Kingdom , even though "You Yourself, Your Majesty, had appeared to me with Your indescribable love…It is so awful to remember it "(W50, 3,4).

With this St Gregory reminds us that his cruel self-annihilation is not about misanthropy, but it is rather a subtle sobriety . *The repentance is a bitter cup, which is like a medicine healing our souls*, no matter how unpleasant it can be.

The human in Narek is standing in front of Christ on a solid and equal ground, and this prayer book is like a smithy where the new person is being hammered.

If we are perfectly sober in spirit, we feel a shame only, for against the perfect heroism, love, and loyalty of Christ we have nothing to show from our part, and our biography can not be compared with Christ's biography, which He had chosen and guided . Against the Bread of Life, we have but the "barley of animals" (W33,1). In fact, we are essentially never in communion with the presence of God in full, following His example in full.

The examination of our soul, on the other hand, shows that the human ill-will is nothing more but just a limitation of goodness, inability to understand the imperfectness, stupidity – when we do not apply efforts to do our best, as our consciousness dictates. That is why a greatest virtue is to realize, that our ability to be good is imperfect, especially because we are prone to be proud when we do good.

Narek highlights the perfection of God as a perfect goodness, but it also highlights that man is not a perfect evil, as the devil is, on the contrary, the evil is not essential for human and it is contrary to his nature;

the evil is a result of mind, inspired by the dark powers of fallen spirits.

Through the faith In Christ all roots of human vices and evil inclinations can be eradicated. And the goal of Narek is "to build the edifice of faith," for when we assess the value of virtues, the faith will be the highest and the paramount, because "only through the faith we are able to approach the sacred mysteries" (W 10,1).

St. Gregory highly esteems also the virtue of wisdom, through which we acknowledge God, through which we love, and we hope. And when the saint sees himself worthless, that is when God turns him most worthy, because there can not be self-prizing, self-crediting, when man exults God. The prize of such soul is the actual presence of God, which is granted to such soul for his humility and meekness.

Humility does not mean to tolerate evil deeds committed against God, as heresies, as excusing crimes, as worshiping demons, as being "nice" for the sake of fake humanism .

The true Christian is a lam of Christ – in his confession, penance, love for God- yet, he is a lion for the world, a soldier, who is eager to establish God's justice, glory, and truth in the world- striving to the martyrdom.

Every page of Narek is a manifestation of the martyrdom, where St. Gregory does not spare himself, declaring the truth about himself against himself, disclosing the very nature , which is adverse to God.

We have God's enemy working inside us, and we have also God's enemy working in the world; we have therefore two fronts to battle in.

If we are evil and imperfect, it is preferable to be as mischievous child – naïve and harmless in our lacks.

And when St. Gregory asks God for graces and virtues, he does not do it in order to feel good about himself for his own glory and fame, when possessing the grace- he rather is longing for the source of grace "to see the Donor."

We have the seal of our baptism, or we have the seal of Caesar imprinted on our souls. If we have a seal of our baptism , we pay all our debts- deliberating us from the cooperation with sins, from sinful inclinations, sinful institutions- and we keep our soul independent and free. Meanwhile if we have the seal of Caesar, we yearn after power, fame, social status, and wealth – to be the prince of this world, which wage is a death. And at this point we can not serve to seals, two masters- God and Caesar (Luke 15).

In Narek we see a human who has these two seals, serving two masters, having two images- God's and Caesar's . Knowing Christ, the Christian serves Caesar, very often because of his weakness rather than ill will. He is deceived, duped, he is confused, he is unable to swim against current – his will succumbs. It is because, unlike Caesar's people, the Christian can not act as powerful, for he is not, can not act as ruler, for he is not, can not set standards, for he has none, can not gain a glory, for he is deprived of any. All a Christian can do is to obey the law of God and to make that law as a basis for human civilization. All which Caesar can do a Christian can not .

If man serves Christ , he serves all.

The Narek is breathing with this truth; Christ and antichrist in man, this inner struggle, this inner antagonism, and the tragedy as its consequence. The image of Caesar in us is our old man fighting the new one, the likeness of a new man in Christ with the old man in Caesar (W 39,1).

This likeness and kinship of our new image with the old one, the status of our soul in duality, are depicted with poetic exclusive genius;

"Torn palm tree ,

Turbid wine ,

Sinking ship,

Smashed pearl,

Milk, poured on ashes…"

Narek is a stentorian eulogy dedicated to God and humanity; it is also the eulogy of the tragedy of the last mankind, a tragedy which ennobles man exalting him to divine, turning this process into universal culture.

It is not about the scarcity of philanthropy in social science, which Narek raises - but it is about efforts through which man is "kept perpetually in justice, " which seems impossible. The tragedy of Narek is a consequence of man's inability to sojourn in this perpetual righteousness.

No matter how profound is the repentance of St. Gregory, no matter how deep is the tragedy caused by the absence of God, St. Gregory never counts his penance to be satisfactory;

"I did not eat ashes for bread,
I did not soak my pillow in my tears,
I did not starve enough in fasts to adhere food, or faint from hardship" (W61,1).

Only in such self-mortification our senses will be cleaned up and will reach the permanent righteousness, as it was achieved by great saints .

But we are not in saints' rank. Then, where is our place? Do we pursue our goal with hypocrisy and ruse, with self deception and inveracity?

"You fulfill the arch of staving moon, or You make it thin ,
You use even its dim light to show us
That You can enrich too our staving bodies in lack of goodness
To make it a perfect ring." (W63, 2).

Nothing is impossible to God who educed all existences from nothing , and if we have nothing but our mortal life- worn out, lethargic, dopy, broken, tearful, despondent, ashamed, darkened- in its course of this earthly journey, if we trust in God, our life can be transformed into a celebration , and we can be sober in heart, brilliant in our image , meek in our mode, joyful in peace, united in love, fearless-obtaining the immortal life of immense light ....In such renascence we confess, above our wretched and fallen state, the Name of Jesus, exulting Father and Son- the Holy Trinity of Spirit (W63,3).

When we constantly glorify God, this our capacity is granted by God, allowing us to know Him and exult Him- and this is the greater perfection man can achieve.

Therefore, according to Narek, the human true virtue is not a *constant state, but a constant objective, and it is an abiding glorification of God* .

Therefore, we are exempt of every virtue under the seal of Adam's shame, because when we examine deep inside us, we see that shame tends "to satisfy the needs of our nature" only – and when we fight unrelenting against that nature- we restore in us the image of God, proving our eminence as humans (W65,1).

We hear Adam's lamentation from Narek's pages, for once being face to face with God, living with God, Adam was deserted and abandoned for his disloyalty afterward.

God has left us. And there are moments of rational illuminations when we fully perceive the fact, and then the whole existence of humanity turns into a Manuscript of Tragedy .

We are under the tyranny of our body, and no matter how much we are being cooked in repentances and restricting laws, we never get the original perfect image of Adam, when he was in Paradise, "unless we exit from our bodies, when time comes "(W69, 1).

Even if we were able to reach the utmost perfection, it would be only in the limits of human nature, which is nothing. Even saints all could do was that they could stand up quickly on their feet when they fell, always exceeding their human nature, keeping it in strict vigilance (W71, 3).

The miraculous healing power of Narek emanates from his ability to magnify meticulously all sins possible for humans, evaluating the "small things, which have value if a great evil," because all is being assessed by the high standards of God -turning man to the court of a wiseacre God" (W72, 2).

St. Gregory Narekatsi does not see his teaching as grand, for no matter how much he learns, yet he never reaches the perfect science of wisdom (W71, 2).

God is perfect- all the rest is imperfect, and his own teaching St. Gregory describes to be high and low momentums , when he "from highest wisdom in one instance can go back to the lowest point, to what he really is " (W71, 2).

The ultimate accord of Narek sounds as a plea – "Let You write my manuscript with Your wisdom, in order it to be a good wage of asceticism " (W85,1). And the good wage is the humility, in which we are kept bent, staring at the earth, where we will be buried as mortals – in full understanding of our material nature , in full readiness to kneel and to bow our heads to the ground before God, worshiping Him in simple way, in true way, not in sophisticated abstruse terms. The simple faith, pure heart will make us to be winners of Heavenly crown (W86, 1).

Narek is touching the space of God. It can be presented as one genuine cry from the depths of heart, each and every chapter of it- as a microcosmic tragedy of human melted in macrocosmic glory of God, in sacred illumination of the human reason, in the divine LOGOS- Christ,

"The Just Light uncreated–
Who establishes everywhere
The life in grace
And the resurrection of just in Christ" (W 97, 1).

Yerevan, 1989-1993

CPSIA information can be obtained
at www.ICGtesting.com
Printed in the USA
LVOW10s1739010217

522883LV00015B/1400/P